AF214600

www.krisfelti-buch-und-lyrik.de
First edition February 2021
© Copyright of the poems: lies with the respective authors
© Copyright of the Illustrations: Kris Felti
Cover Design: Dream Design Cover and Art, Renee Rott
© Kris Felti

Verlag & Druck: tredition GmbH,
Halenreie 40-44, 22359 Hamburg
978-3-347-15055-3 (Paperback)
978-3-347-15056-0 (Hardcover)
978-3-347-15057-7 (eBook)

Kris Felti and friends

Sing with me

Beyond national borders

Thank you so much to all poets

who joined me

Prologue to the volume of poetry

"Art is tenderness for our soul!"
In the year of the corona pandemic in particular, we became painfully aware of how lonely distance can be. Distance from our families and friends, distance from countries we like to travel to. While wars and refugee disasters have touched us in the past few years, it is now a catastrophe that affects us all and everything: social systems, the economy, education, be it at kindergartens, schools and universities. Everywhere, on every continent, we are fighting the same enemy, a virus that has shown us how vulnerable and alike we are. We are people of this one planet, with the same fears, feelings, hopes and dreams. Only our cultures are different. But it is precisely this otherness that makes our life together so valuable and enriching. With the volume of poetry "Sing with me, beyond national borders", poets and writers from different nations around the world speak with one voice. Continents grow together with our songs, which each have their own melodies, but the same rhythm of our hearts. I thank all the poets and writers who took part in the project: Arijit Misra, Aziza Dahdouh, Michael Morrissey, San Lin Tun, Gary Steven Corseri, Milka Minkova, Lyonga Michael Justin Mushaga, Jillani Birech, Christian Nae, Sascha Helck, Devi Maya Pradhan, Ishmail Kamara, Joanna Janosz, Keith Hyland, Lucia V. Cleaeno, Laseeta Kunhikannan, Melissa Medina, Yhohannah Holm, Suhani Jain,Samar Bhowmick and Mladen M. Tokić. This book of poems would not exist without you.All the best and stay healthy.

February, 2021 Kris Felti

Sing With Me!

(Kris Felti)

Sing with me!
Beyond national borders
from continent to continent.
Unity in feeling and doing
makes bad sentiments wither.
Because we have the same dream
the same concern
the same courage
the same enemy.

Sing with me!
Our diversity
raises the curtain
narrow-minded doubt.
Scenery of our similarities,
spotlight
of our fragility,
legacy of our
humanity.

Sing with me!

Peace

(Gary Steven Corseri)

There was a point we were drifting towards;
There was a place we were seeking.

We called it: The Home of Sublime Understanding,
The Quality of Differences Subtly Restored.

"After the War," we assured one another:
The War to Make Living Safe for the Living;
The War we have been breathing since birth—and
before.

But the War never ended.
Its sand filled our mouths with reproachable sorrows.

It was mother and father, sister and brother;
Priest and rabbi, preacher and imam.

The Causes lay under a quilt of stars.
And numerous corpses clawed the hard ground.

The politicians hallowed the ground.
The various preachers hallowed the ground.
Children placed wreaths on hallowed ground.
Great monuments were built on hallowed ground.
They gleamed in the sun.
Patterned, colored cloths, called flags, flapped

Over hallowed ground.
The band played anthems over hallowed ground.

And we forgot:

There was a point we were drifting towards;
There was a place we were seeking;
We called it: The Home of Sublime Understanding,
The Quality of Differences Subtly Restored.

Deafening Song

(Arijit Misra)

I could hear,
the dead leaf falling on the ground.
The Caterpillar munching leaf,
burped.

You're cutting the tree and I could hear
Her screaming,
The birds cursing,
Gush of warm pale yellow blood rolling.

I could hear
the dew dropped on grass,
hear her splattered.
You stood on them.
I could hear them crying,
stomped insects cursing.
I couldn't hear you sing amidst all this sound.

Where Incessant Laughter Resounds
(San Lin Tun)

No matter whom we are and where we live,
We live in a one world as a unit entity.
Don't grudge hatred and breed discrimination against
each other,
Cos' they are not suited to us.
We are a breed of humans, with minds and passions,
We need to help and love each other.
To build a better place and a better world,
We have to strive with our might with fervour.
When you see and want to smell a flagrant flower,
Just remember that others will also want to inhale it.
Spread that good news to others,
Then, they will be rejoiced and rewarded.
Don't hold things tight only in your hand as if it were
your own,
Crush your ego. Instead, you need to share what you
have with others.
Simply, we call it an expression of humanity and
empathy,
Caring, sharing, and loving are a noble feature of human
beings.
Diversity is noticeably a beauty as sparking as diamonds,
It is also a blessing for us too.
Cherishing and nourishing that humane spirit,
Incessant soft laughter will resound in the world.

Message Of Peace

(Milka Minkova)

Summer seagull white,
summer high,
high in the non-smooth width
to carry a message of freedom
and peace.

Everywhere in the world
instead of bombs
to sow flowers
and no one
not to suffer anymore.

To live in harmony and peace
light to shine through the celestial expanse
a smile to be shed on every child,
to grow in peace, like a May flower

Summer, white gull
summer high in the sky,
carry this message
for freedom and peace.

Fused into one
to all brothers
peacefully in the world
let our days pass

No hungry mouths
for a crust of bread suffering
To live in love and happiness
we long for that peace

Anuchanda: Salvation

(Samar Bhowmick)

Let humanity be a contagious disease
For the universe
Civilization survives as heaven
Human not products.

Be blesses creation
May humanity be enlightened
Let people be friends with animals
Let man be god.

The distinction between men and women is broken
Let the people be on their knees
Overcoming the darkness of all civilizations
Let Anu be illuminated.

Be valued in mother's compassion
Of father, brother, sister
To break human apart
Be enlighten knowledge fire.

Let the people bow down to God
Like their religion
God forbid
Violence as hatred.

Let the human soul wake up

Affection for love
Human life is never in vain
Bless the creation.

Equal affection in all creation
Donate when done
God keeps the heavens happy
Breath will save.

Hail, Sol Invictus.

(Michael Morrissey)

Pray tell what mortal hand or eye
could frame such irony,
read from the inside:
'Jedem das Seine'.
We will not tolerate
outrageous conspiracy theories.
Preemptive war
and torture
will set you free.
On this drizzle of a day
the old god struggles
across cluttered cyber skies
fortunately returning
but still the iron stands.
It does not melt like buildings
struck by airplanes
or vaporize or sink into the earth
like airplanes
on certain days.
Reason is but a mode the mind abides in.
The rest is dark, like blood.

A Transporter

(Aziza Dahdouh)

A human being
An important element in the chain of life
Call my name and I will respond
I AM present...I AM present
Not giving up to my role
Nor denying to my mission
Actually no plans for retirement
I AM present soul and heart
I AM a unique creation
My chromosome says that
I AM a Transporter of data(DNA)
From my ancestors to the next generation
I existed centuries ago
And I will survive since there is life
I was my first grandma and
I will be my next granddaughter
I am a strong bridge
I AM a circle of life
And who created me will protect me
No one can tamper with my genetic characteristics
I AM a whole library
A lot of data stored within me
Ignored by myself
On a strict mission
No need to go back to the age of caves
Come, together hand in hand

Let's help those who need help
Let's feed those who are hungry
Let's shelter those who are homeless
We were not created in vain
We are The Caliph of Allah on Earth,
distinguished by the Almighty.

I think Back Again

(Sascha Helck)

Oh my heart, it is so difficult.
Do you see them, the old spruce trees at the beginning of
the forest, their needles green and their bark filling the
air with resin like never before?
Behind her green wall I have experienced, loved, suffered,
laughed and cried a lot and it seems as if something is
still there.
Something from back then.

Behind the wall, in the old log cabin that we know so
well, yes there, you hear a voice, almost loud.
Is it the past that speaks there?
Did my longing for old times call you and there is
something in sight for me?
An experience that no one has had before.
A breath, no, more than that, a gust of wind, full of
emotions,
Joy and love caused by my feelings, I brood.

Can this really be me again for a brief?
For a one Moment see the ghosts of the past and I return
to the beautiful moments?
Is that possible?

Carefully and slowly, I approach the beginning of the
forest.

Rotten twigs crack under my soles, make me a little
nervous, but I don't feel fear.
Just a little longer ... Made it, I'm here. The log cabin.
I stopped and looked at her.

But the shrill sound of the cock's cry pulled me out of my
beautiful dream and let me look into the here and now.
You can't go back, old boy!
You can't dream about it as much as you want!
Past is past.
But one day there will be a reunion
with everything that was dear to you.
You will see.

Let Me Be Extinct Too

(Arijit Misra)

I am freezing my eggs before it's too late to conceive.
Not knowing when I'll find a lover.
And not even ready now, with time chances may deceive.

Wish I could also freeze the eggs of the pelicans giving
eggs near my door.
I don't see the sparrows chirping any more.

If I could freeze the eggs of the tiger giving cubs in the
forest.
I don't see the vultures eating leftovers as the guest.

Hope I could freeze the eggs of the cuddly Panda scarce
on this cruel planet.
I don't hear the macaw aping my voice like a sonnet.

Wish I could freeze the eggs of the stingray before there
are no more.
Dolphins are not swimming in the river behind my house
any more.

Wish I could freeze the eggs of them before they all are
going to die.
Are you still looking for icy mammoths just to say: hi?

Blame

(Arijit Misra)

I often blame you,
And you blame me too.
Things may go wrong never realized by we two.

I blame the government and I do it again.
They blame me for not doing my part for their cause just slain.

I blame my parents for not having wealth.
They blame me for the state of their ill health.

I blame my son for not putting effort what I wish he shall.
He blames me for not being rich like the papa of his pal.

I blame my boss for always being pushy.
He blames me for being laid back and lazy.

I blame my Neighbor for being too loud.
He blames me when my stature touches the cloud.

I blame the beggar when she asks for a coin.
She blames me for nothing on her loin.

It's a game we all play whenever we fail.
Like a fleeing dog, between legs tucking its tail.

With both palms you clap,
Look at you before the blame you slap.

Little Human

(Kris Felti)

Wonder of nature
Coronation of the Empress
who directs the flow of life.
Apparently inconspicuous
and part of the contract
to immortality
your little hands intervene
in my life.
Time as a silent admonisher
weaves our threads
to patterns,
which are unique in their blaze of colors.
You are my teacher,
my soul doctor,
my drive on difficult terrain.
And if your pattern changes
cross with other threads,
as a source to a new stream,
are you fulfilling my legacy
Because then I'll be with you
Always there
for eternity.

Sing With Me

(Jillani Birech)

Sing with me,
Sing loudly,
Let's your voice be heard;
Come out of your cocoon,
Juice your brain
And utter your words;
Let them know
You're here and there;
Let them recognise
You're quiet,
But your words
And your ideas
Are heard
Let them know
Your quietness doesn't
Mean you're absent;
Let's cross the borders,
And tell the world
We're here and there.

My Egypt

(Kris Felti)

Dipped in orange
wrapped in a thousand colorful cloths,
are you my fairy tale,
my longing.
Captured by tender veils,
from scents and tones,
never known,
very familiar,
I strip off what I know to believe.
Indigenous habits
and educated prejudices
dissolved,
like kissed morning dew.
And dancing, in rustling silk
they combine to form a symphony
from the sounds of ancient cultures.
Strange familiar present,
and a boundless love,
that knows no national borders.

For you and Kathmandu

(Lucia V. Celaeno)

Abducted by sand drifts of time and space,
Eternally trapped in the rhythm of this seraphic place.

Dreams of thundering cascades
Mountains and forests
Where racket and silence go hand in hand
Hooting cars and slumbering cows sharing street life
Sadhus and monks praying in spiritual meditation
Dogs straying, children playing
Waiting for the sunset caress to fall over Nepal.

Monkeys agile, curious and insolent
Grabbing food, bags and phones
Sunshine and laughter, lingering
Every day amazing, surprising
Monsoon and rainbows
Hovering over scented mustard fields
Waking up in the arms of Nepal.

Kathmandu love
My desire will always be with you
Yet, I know deep in my heart
I will never see you.

City of peace and ancient temples
Palaces, fountains and dreamful gardens

Festivals and celebrations
Decorations of 'Sayapatri' strings
Flaming red, orange and yellow vanishing
Absorbed by the chaotic traffic-jam
Enchanted by the smiles of Nepal

Electric wiring dangerously knotted
Like rusty, festoon cobwebs overhead
Power cuts and broken range
Pollution haze and clouds of dust
Washed away by nature's rain
Fostered by dearth, the erratic strength
Entrenched in the roots of Nepal.

Kathmandu love
My desire will always be with you
Still, I know deep in my heart
I will never touch you.

Religion and culture, closing like an invisible seal
The secret heritage of the never-ending Karma wheel
Himalaya, enticing goddess covered in eternal snow
Watching over valleys and hills
Spreading her wondrous beauty
Hiding treasures and myths
Bewildering infinity of awesome Nepal.

Land of Buddha's colorful mantras
Happiness and prayers carried on a breeze of wind
Powerful wishes great and small
For rich and poor, for old and young

Passionate and sincere
Heartbeats travelling everywhere
Embraced by the warmth of Nepal.

Kathmandu love
My desire will always be with you
Now, carved deep in my heart
I will never forget you.

Mysterious Love

(Devi Maya Pradhan)

Love, thou art the Sirius,
The golden pheasant and the rose,
I was gleeful, a little curious
Content with whom I chose.
Thou single sight fill me with pleasure
Thrilling as a twisty roller coaster ride;
Like the glorious shining treasure
Demurred was I by thy side.
Thou possessed the bizarre aura,
That made me adhere with thee,
Thy fragrant tantamount to flora
Got me sink in the insanity.
Let's ignite the love of ours
Let it be immortal
We shall rejoice for tranquil hours
With these bountiful chortle.

Savings

(Samar Bhowmick)

Believe Anu
I have nothing
Without the poet's love
Nothing.

The bond between humanity and love
There is nothing else
The poet has no house
There is no happiness
No regrets
No intelligence
There is not even a shortage.

The poet has no boundaries of his own
No lies
No mask
No friends
There is no enemy
There is no selfishness
There is no useful life in civilization.

The poet has no desire for conditions
No sudden dreams
There is no destruction
You don't have
Not after

There is no abundance
And there is no narrowness.

The poet does not have thoughts devoid of conscience
No doubt
There is no despair
No sleep
No Sis
No tricks
There is no expectation of receipt.

The poet is not afraid
There is no decay
There is no arrogance
There is no greed
No rate
There is no victory
There is no competition in rat race

English Weather
(Joanna Janosz)

English weather
Rain rain
Down the drain
Cats and dogs
In the street
Very nice indeed.
'Agatha Christie'
Misty blood blood
In the street
Very nice indeed
Rain rain blood blood
She was a little slut
Knife knife in the street
Very nice indeed
Bond my name is Bond
In the street
Astor Martin very nice indeed
Forgive me my immigrant's spleen.
God save the Queen

We're So Far, And Yet So Close

(Lyonga Micheal Justin Mushaga)

Never in my craziest dreams did I ever imagined that
someone who has never seen me knows me so well.
We're so far, and yet so close.
I fear calls and texts from strangers and people I know,
But I get unstable if I don't receive one from you.
It's only on mobiles, but when we talk it's like we're in
the same sit.
We're so far, and yet so close.
Race, color and background are just words to us.
The people around me make me so anxious, unable to
open up to anyone.
With you I can be myself and vent freely. you don't just
vent too, but listen to me.
A stranger, but so trustworthy.
We're so far, and yet so close.
How is it that me and a stranger are so close?
It's like there's no hate in the world.
We're so fay, and yet so close.
Facebook, Instagram and Twitter are our mediums.
But our hearts connect deeper.
I still wish for when we'll not be far but really close.

Sing with me

(Christian Nae)

Let's sing a song,
In one word.
In the sweet language of peace
Like the angels of Heaven.

Let's speak a language,
All over the earth.
Sweet words of love,
Let it be our song.

Come sing with me,
Indian Brother,
And you German,
And you Mexican

Come and take a seat,
Good English brother
Brother from Morocco
And you Chinese.

You have an Arab brother,
Take the Bulgarian too
The Turk, the Tatar,
In Serbian and Hungarian.

Let's sing a song.

In one word.
In the sweet tongue of peace,
Like the angels of Heaven.

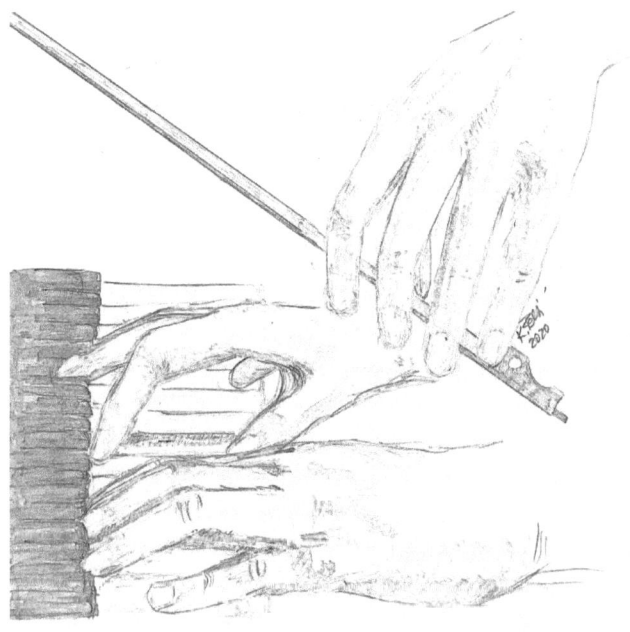

Heroes

(Gary Steven Corseri)

Do not call them "heroes"
if they have done your killing for you.
Say that they have done your bidding;
say they were your "soldiers."

Say that you have trained them well:
They are the oiled machinations of war,
performing as expected.

Refrain from saying "professionals,"
and the usual nonsense about "surgical strikes."
They were never doctors and nurses
in starched, white linens.

The best heroes are dead ones—
mortified and mortared.
They neither complain nor contradict.
They don't re-live "friendly fire" incidents,
the sonofabitch sergeant-sadist,
nor the rapist in their midst.
They don't see again
the faces of traumatized children.
Their bones stretch to attention under the sod.

The man and woman who will kill and injure
because some fool tells them to
are just little spin-off fools.

No act born of ignorance is heroic.
Heroes are sensible, not imbeciles.
They dispel myths; they neither create
nor perpetuate them.

The fully manifested hero,
aware of his power and dignity,
is more than human, is humane.

Heroes don't talk about heroes.
They need no confetti showered in their faces.
They question; they learn; they challenge; they act
according to their own honed principles:

What is truth? for example;
what is honor?

It Is Not Night Yet

(Kris Felti)

It is not night yet
when dark shadows dance ominously
and the crying child
looks for the mother.
Tender plants in the quiet garden
cherished and cared for,
and some delicious fruit.

It is not night yet
when cold winds do not carry the seed
and fatherly care
leads to nowhere.
High walls protrude into the blue.
Lost the green
no light it touches.

It is not night yet
when thunderous gout licks the reefs,
and the fire of the tower
makes the horizon wide.
Patriots' feelings were rubbed off.
Forgotten betrayed
Humanity.

It is not night yet
when the human is
aware of his mortality,
that boundaries, created in minds and wars,
are not safe boundaries
for life.

Gone

(Arijit Misra)

I used to laugh
riding the huge waves,
And the road she used to pave.
I used to love her the way she wanted,
With my song she used to be enchanted.

I used to see her face so dear,
Often beyond till I could see her.
I can't see now at a distance,
Nor she is there in the abundance.

I used to ride with her in those flights,
She used to show me the way of light.
I cant ride now with the body so frail,
Nor she's there to blaze the trail.

Where's the wave I used to ride? Where's the hand that
used to guide?
Where's the song I used to sing?
Where's the heart I was attached with a string?

Gone are my days,
Lost in a stack of hay.
I'm left with nothing but me,
And a broken heart always ready to flee"

Age of Innocence
(Devi Maya Pradhan)

Beauty of innocence, how cheery to cherish,
Age of innocence how tenderly flourish;
Blissful heart with serene mind,
Abundance of pleasure, truly one of a kind.
Sparkling the daughterly smile
From moonly face, distinctive style,
No hatred, no arrogance, no anger burning;
Merely love of innocence eyes adorning.
A little child, heaven sent angel
Blessing everyone desires so special,
None mislikes the toddler behavior,
Thanks to almighty, redeemer and savior.
With no worries what future has in its store,
Chuckling of her is what all adore;
In the melody of soothing lullaby,
Sunny little eyes world's glorify.
Longing for ten thousand miles to go,
Seeds of prosperity to sow,
Eradicating the worldly ego but love!
Unfurling peace as a sailing dove!

Defeat

(Samar Bhowmick)

Still
Defeated life
Even if I don't have it
In the ultimate reality of civilization
Love is like the wind
The polluted air of the industrial world.

Although the modern world is rich in industry
People could not be artistic
Love takes in the breath
Believes
Exhales.

Although love for life
The invisible untouchable is formless
For Anu, for civilization
Always new.

In the regular thoughts of the gentlemen
Life is for survival
Thousands of naked dreams for life,
So

Want more accessories.

Raindrops for storms

So for the body
For the dream to compete
For honor in civilization
The head is like a conventional coin
I want a little fire.

Love is burning for lack of fire
Anu, life and poetry
Even if love is successful
Defeat life in the end
Music Poetry and Poet.

When Pavarotti died

(Gary Steven Corseri)

When Pavarotti died
No Statesman made a statement.
(They were embarrassed by their voices.)
No Officer of Meddling meddled
In another man's affairs.
The skylarks fell from their windows.
(They had been admiring
Their own reflections.
Now they cried in unison, "He's gone.")
Rudolfo wept; Bellini beat his temples.
There was no war anywhere worth celebrating—
No victories, no monuments
Remotely compensating
The people for their loss.
"O mio babbino caro,"
Sang a hundred forlorn women.
Somewhere in a forest
A leaf fell from a redwood,
Undulating downward
Until it folded itself in humus.
Fox eyes narrowed and glowed in moonlight.
Every feral creature bowed.

Our Voice Dedicated to Kathmandu

(Ishmail Kamara)

Voices from the mountain top will echo
and manifest and strive and impact our world
with positivity.

Never shall we weep again
for the darker days are over

Light of fortune will rise and shine
and light up the mountain top till the valley
and restore our spirituality

The clear blue sky is not only blue
It represents our strength and brings us hope

On hope, we shall hang on like a rope
which will remain firm till we shout, Salvation!
Yes! Salvation is here at the mountain top
and is here to stay.

Our voices will be free.
Our values will be restored.
Our dreams will come true.

The echo of our voice will shed a little tear of joy
We shall keep on calling from the mountain top,
till all our calls are answered.

You Are My Me

(Kris Felti)

From the beginning a dance for two
to the beat of the innate melody.
Timid steps in a gentle caress
and unshakable security.
The cold breath of loneliness
stays for a very long time
in front of a closed door.
Affectionate gang
braided in red and blue,
determine the rhythm of the heart.
As if in a rustling
in the song of the woods,
we grow and grow up
to find in waltz or in melancholy
alone that melody
that promises uniqueness.
We are two fragments
soul-wounded,
aware of the loss of our destiny,
to be one with each other.
Missing for life
don't let go of our hand.
You are my me,
and dancing to my own tune
I always dance you too.
confusingly,
and yet
unmistakable symphony.

»Dance of twins«

Last Play
(Arijit Misra)

I see
Fog in a distance
Covered bodies
I see
Twisted moon
Feeling pain
I see
Pieces of cloud
Wiping her
I know the tears

I hear
Stars mourning
They're sad
Dogs sing along
I hear the dogs crying
I know they're sad

I see
Droplets on leaf
I see tears
I see snow
I know it is filling the graves
I feel
Wind blowing
Widows whispering

I feel
Chill in air
I know souls are there

I know
Me and my dog only watch the play
I know who's conducting the piece.

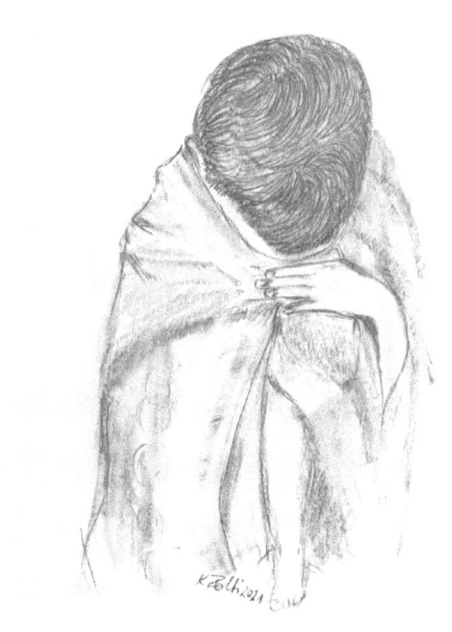

The 'Peace Process' Dies Again

(Gary Steven Corseri)

There is no 'peace process'.
There is peace... and the absence of peace—
The gnawing hunger for it,
The desperation of the vanquished.

Does the peace dove fly with a shattered wing?
The shattered wing is the wing of war.
War is a sieve capturing humanity.
Blood seeps out of the mouths of the sieve.

How does one speak to a four-year-old child
Of processes, politics, quid pro quos?
No mother dresses the wounds of the child.
Her mother's eyes stare in wonder forever.

And we wonder: Do laws since time immemorial,
All proclamations, all declarations
Matter in the eyes of a hurt, dying child?
Have men proven their manhood again in her eyes?

Fools in high places clamor for war; fools follow,
Fearing not following. Platitudes murder
For the sake of murdering—for fools
In high places and fools following.

No one dare speak the Truth of the soul.
The tax-paying herd takes succor in soccer.
My team, my tribe, my country, myself—nothing
Else matters, no one else counts, unseeing

The eyes of a child looking in wonder:
What did she do to bring on such anger?
What did her mother do, staring forever?
Why is her father so still in the rubble?

War crimes and genocide, honor, dishonor.
Where to begin, where does it end?
All the entanglements—hatred and loving.
The State... The Nation... The People... The--

How does one speak to a four-year-old child
Of processes, politics, quid pro quos?
With all the lexicons, all the professors—
No one has learned the language of children.

O TEMPORA!

O MORES!

(Mladen M. Tokić)

Where to go
time is a jackal
time of river rains
sleepless nights
enraged beasts
of lost loves
it is a time of hatred
in the time of drugs and gamblers
it is a time of poverty

O TEMPORA!
O MORES!

It's pandemic time
suffering
a time of invisible war
animal morals
which pairs under the walls
of this time
under rotting lead
stone wormholes
in bones
in the bosom

O TEMPORA!
O MORES!

Which is why the suffering of the world
is love hard to sing
in the customs of the human race
and the bastard of the cosmic to live
to stay
in dusty books
on the dilapidated
pages of time
to travel
chase through the night
die at the cells
to leave forever

O TEMPORA!
O MORES!

Where to go
goodbye is death
whether to live
to live is more beautiful

Butcher Shop

(Michael Morrissey)

Vince says I was courageous to avoid that butcher shop.
Which makes me as courageous as Bill Clinton,
Dan Quayle, and 60% of the rest of my generation.

Bob says he was a fool to go to war,
and Tim O'Brien (in The Things They Carried)
even says he was a coward.

Well thanks, fellows, but no thanks.
I may be a coward, but I won't be a liar and a hypocrite.

They were brave.
I was not.

Bravery is when the man says,
"Put your ass here, no matter what,"
and you put it there.

They thought it was right, and so they went.
That took guts.
I wouldn't take that from them, even if I could.
No, I salute them, especially the ones like Bob
and Ron Kovics and Oliver Stone and the VVAW
who first said yes, and then said no
and thus were two times brave.
I'll turn out for their parade, anytime.

I thought it was wrong, so I didn't go.
That wasn't guts.
I would have gone to Canada, but I lied at the physical
and lucked out, then lucked out again on the lottery,
the same one the President lucked out on.
Was that guts?

I checked a few wrong boxes on the questionnaire
and got in to see the shrink. I didn't think I had a chance,
any more than I'd had to pass the CO test.
"Tell me about your mother," the shrink said.
I couldn't believe it. I'd read some Freud, too.
"Well, she's very attractive..." I began,
and looked distraught, which wasn't hard at all.
I had a beard then, too, which might have helped.
Or maybe he just wanted to give me a break.

Then I found a civilian shrink to confirm the diagnosis--
"Schizoid blah blah blah"--meaning the war was crazier
than I was.
A "mass neurosis," the doctor called it.
A great understatement, I thought.

Smart? No, not hardly.
The smart ones, like Bill and Dan, played their cards
better
and made it to the White House, where they can fight
their wars
in comfort, with no blood, no pain,
and no guilt. After all, the people elected them.
I was just lucky.

Now about stupidity.
Bob says it was a stupid war
and how could they have been so stupid?
That was my question, too, a long time ago
and then I buried it, because there was no answer.

I could believe that Johnson was a stupid man (not true)
and that Nixon was just plain depraved (true)
and that my countrymen were patriots
because that's how we were brought up.

But what about those Harvard guys—
the Bundies, the Rostows, the Kissingers,
the best and the brightest, the Whiz Kids?
I knew I wasn't smarter than they were.
I couldn't even get into Harvard.

But any child could see it.
The national security at stake in Vietnam?
Not even close.
"Saving face," they called it, in the end
and more tens of thousands died
conquering nothing, defending nothing,
least of all us, or freedom and democracy
under slimeball dictators named Ngo and Ky and Thieu
whose names were as unspeakable as they were.

"Hell Ngo, we won't go!" was my only answer then.
I could never get my mouth around the other stuff, like
"Hey, hey, LBJ, how many kids did you kill today!"
Weren't we all Americans, somewhere down the line?

How could our own government be the enemy?
Absurd.

But how could they be so stupid, when they weren't?

An unnecessary war, and they refused to stop.
What could be more stupid, or immoral?
Then, as Bob says, they added stupidity to stupidity
and didn't fight it properly.

How could they be so stupid?

There was no answer, so I stopped asking.
Then finally it ended, and the historical consensus grew
like grass over the graves: "A well-intentioned error.
Uncle Sam is innocent, Uncle MacGeorge and Uncle
Henry
and all the other uncles, on the grounds of stupidity.
They didn't know the war would cost so much—
$570 billion, accounting for inflation,
and all those lives. How tragic."

But my question was never answered.

Until I saw Jack's head snap back
and all that blood come out of my TV set.
I knew then, because I was hit
and nothing hits that hard but the truth.
I couldn't prove it, but I didn't have to.
I was my own Exhibit A.
Later, when I read about JFK's withdrawal plan,

my mind caught up with my gut
and I knew where all the blood was coming from.

It was the blood of my dead brothers.
They had found me.
I felt their pain, which was much greater than my pain,
and their anger, which was much greater than my anger.
I had become a conduit, having tapped somehow a giant
reservoir
of blood and bile deep in the bowels of the earth.
I felt like a volcano, watching itself erupt.

I knew it was them because they found me,
not the other way around. I wasn't even looking.
I was sound asleep. Never had the slightest curiosity,
never read a single book or article about the
assassination,
knew nothing of the evidence, never connected it with
the war.
I was a victim, too.
They lost their lives, and I lost my mind,
like Rip Van Winkle, for a quarter of a century.

But I'm back now, motherfuckers.
I know the answer to the question.
It took me 25 years to figure it out
but now I know.

It's the wrong question. They weren't stupid.
They were lying.

Butterfly

(Devi Maya Pradhan)

I stepped on the mown lawn
With the genesis of dawn;
Watching those little valiant soul
Sparkling, precisely cheerful.
My eyes sparkled quite timid
Widely opened dark and humid;
Delighted was me
Happy were my eyes that see.
How beautiful a butterfly is!
With it's amazing flowery _ kiss;
Beating it's wings up and down
Ample of dances it's shown.
Seems so delicate and meek
Yet it's dedicated for Pleasure it seek
It wears the worldly top_ notch colors
That attires it for bountiful hours.
I longed to see it everyday
All my life in every way,
Thought never would it fly away
But alas! "Nothing gold can Stay".

Give alms

(Samar Bhowmick)

Give me alms
The sure human world of triangulation
Respect for Anu is the right to freedom
And for my seniors
Pure love smeared with reverence.

Give me alms
Natural death of trees, plants, leaves, animals and birds
Independent voices, politics, songs, story poems
Constitution of the seventy-two, honor of the red-green
flag
The smile on the face of the starving weak exploited
man.

Give me alms
A little love for Taslima Tanu Abhijit
Civilized breathing for oppressed people
A little knowledge for self-centered barbaric fanatics
The water of thirst instead of the tears of Birangana.

Give me alms
Chandradevi Rabindranath Robert Frost Nazrul
The speaker is Bangabandhu Suryasen CR Dutta
Khudiram Pritilata Nurjahan Begum
Salam Rafiq is the ideal of blessing.

I am an unknown religious poet
Give me alms

A piece of human vision for life
Love for water, love for air
Balanced love for soil and people.

Lost And Found

(Arijit Misra)

Lost the moments in the tub getting bathed by my mother,
And the days trying to ride a bicycle tightly held by my father.

Lost my dearest friend when I was in another town,
Lost my dog with his fur dark brown.

Lost the boyish charm for which your heart started to beat,
Lost the chit of paper with love written on it.

Lost the vigor with which I fought in the war,
And so many unknown faces of the dead soldiers.

Lost the loving touch of you on my heart,
And the pain I felt when you did part.

Lost my son when he flew away with his new-found dove,
And with that lost our bond of love.

Lost my hair too with passing time,
And then the life within like the last dime.

Lost so many things that I lost count,
Only thing I found deep in the forest is my grave mound.

Inside Job

(Michael Morrissey)

1.
The somnambular peregrinations that we like to call the
life of the mind
are seldom interrupted by ideas.
Still, it happens.
A butterfly flaps its wings in Java, causing an earthquake
in the mind.
A bug awakens in some dell of memory and becomes a
colossus,
straddling the continental lobes.
The faintest whistle, growing unheard like the corn,
suddenly house-high,
bursts like a banshee out of the blue-blown sky
and finds us standing in the tracks.
2.
Why weren't the windows closed on Elm Street?
How can a bullet do gymnastics?
How could a caveman beat a multi-billion-dollar air
force?
How could those buildings fall straight down?
We think inside our minds how it could be
that so many could die so strangely
until one tells us, screaming through our deafness
"We didn't die. You did."
What are we but ghosts, waiting to be born?

Weird Kid. Weird Guy.

(Lyonga Micheal Justin Mushaga)

Negative and positive attract. Am that negative that repels.
The Weird Kid. Weird Guy.
Always deferent from the crowd.
The hull class laughs, but I wallow because it's at me they
laugh.
Haha, The Weird Kid, The Weird Guy.
In church everyone listens to God, but I listen to my anxiety.
Weird Kid, Weird Guy.

The world as we know it

(Keith Hyland)

The world as we know it
will never be the same.
Our political leaders have gone mad.
They never bothered
they never will.
Filling pockets there is just a thrill there.
Four homeless people were found dead on our streets today.
Nothing said, just wear a mask.
Draw the right amount of air from your body.
They know what to do there, but are silent.
Mass murder-genocide.
It's not a good time to be alive

Now Float Me Down

(Gary Steven Corseri)

Now float me down from that high town, my love;
For we are born to sorrow, men have said,
And cannot travel where the angels rove;
Now float me down to ground where men have bled.

There, heartache cannot thunder through our skin;
We're drenched to magic, drunken out of time;
The hours dance like refugees between
Our arms; the cool moon's hanging like a dime.

Here, where we're waked by sudden storms of bombs,
The infant's world is strangled with a groan;
Death, perched on crutches, pesters us for alms.
O, do not rush me here, now float me down....

The ghosts of many gunners chafe the ground
Where we dance heart to heart without a sound.

(Making love in a time of war... (for Joy))

Homeless

(Devi Maya Pradhan)

No roof over my tired head
No shelter for my meek body
No food for my hungry soul
None to calm my despair mind!
Travelled the forlorn streets_
Boulevard of broken dreams
Satiated with plight and anguish
Starved for taste of humanity.
The world kicked me off
Out of my comfy home,
Invisible was I, I wonder
When nobody sees me crying.
Few multitudes showed me love
With piece of cake or loaf of bread
Accepted with kindness; bowing _
Heartfelt gratitude I did show.
I am human, they are too
Same blood do we bleed
Why so discrimination? But,
I live in street and they at home!

The Connection

(Melissa Emalia Medina)

I watched the moon with you without knowing you
Our need synchronized thru space and time
I have felt your pain as you have mine

Our individual smallness shrouds oneness
Stardust they call us
Bloodborne of legends and miracles
I
Feel
You

With each breath
Our unity a field of reciprocity
Humanity

I watched the moon with you without knowing you
I've walked with you
Thru space and time
I
Have
Loved
You

The Moon needs no Papers

(Laseeta Kunhikannan)

Gliding through the night
the silvery moon
stopped by my window.
'Any message my dear
to friends- far or near?'
I have sent a quilt to keep you warm
colored in shades of autumn;
And aroma of moist bread
that I dipped in light sauce.
Did you find them?
The moon needs no papers
To go from India to Australia.
Of anklets that ring when I dance,
I have sent some music to you.
Wearing flimsy scarves of indigo
the silvery moon
is carrying some secrets too.
Of the letter I found in my math book
and then of the peacock feather on my desk
Did she tell you all these?
The moon needs no papers
to reach you, you see,
and will meet you soon
outside any window of yours.

Gorrión

(Arijit Misra)

Between us let there be,
Thickly soldiered border,
I would know when your heart grows tender,
I would always remain your secret intruder.

Between us let there be, Incomprehensible barrier of
language,
I will understand you in that haze,
I would talk to you even being in the maze.

Between us let there be,
Strictest of religion standing guard,
For your love I will be standing in a herd,
And would pray for you in your tongue like a nerd.

Between us let there be,
Miles of distance to grow,
I will see the moon that you know,
And I would die for you with a waning her in tow.

But this time I will incarnate
And would love to be a sparrow,
Would love to look at your face through your window,
I wish then I would be loved in your shadow.

75

Your Heart Is My Home

(Kris Felti)

Your heart is my home.
Gentle swells of warm waves
flood me
blush my face
to breathless longing.

Your heart is my happiness
Unrestrained storms of tender touch
light up like a streak of light
on our horizon
to breathless longing.

Your heart is my treasure.
Carried by wide wings
do you spread a world before me
in gold and blue,
to breathless immortality.

Ode To The Women

(Kris Felti)

Sensitive ones,
life giving ones,
unconditionally protective ones,
caregiver ones,
the understanding ones,
called by your profession.
Without you
everything would be in this world
impossible and incomplete.

Neonate

(Samar Bhowmick)

Happy future
Tidy earth
Humanity around the world
Upcoming child is there
The eyes of our delusion
Hopeless frail
But Anu;
On the skeletal idol of cholera
A constant stream of thoughts
How to connect the religion
How to stop the baby in future
The whole empire is in capitalism
Committed to various associations
Fear of that naked newborn
Chase after
This is the edge and edge of the earth
Meeting procession UN
Walk in their way
Born with an irresistible heart
The next nude infant
I am one in the world court
Poor unbearable poet
I want to be independent in the future
And naked neonate.

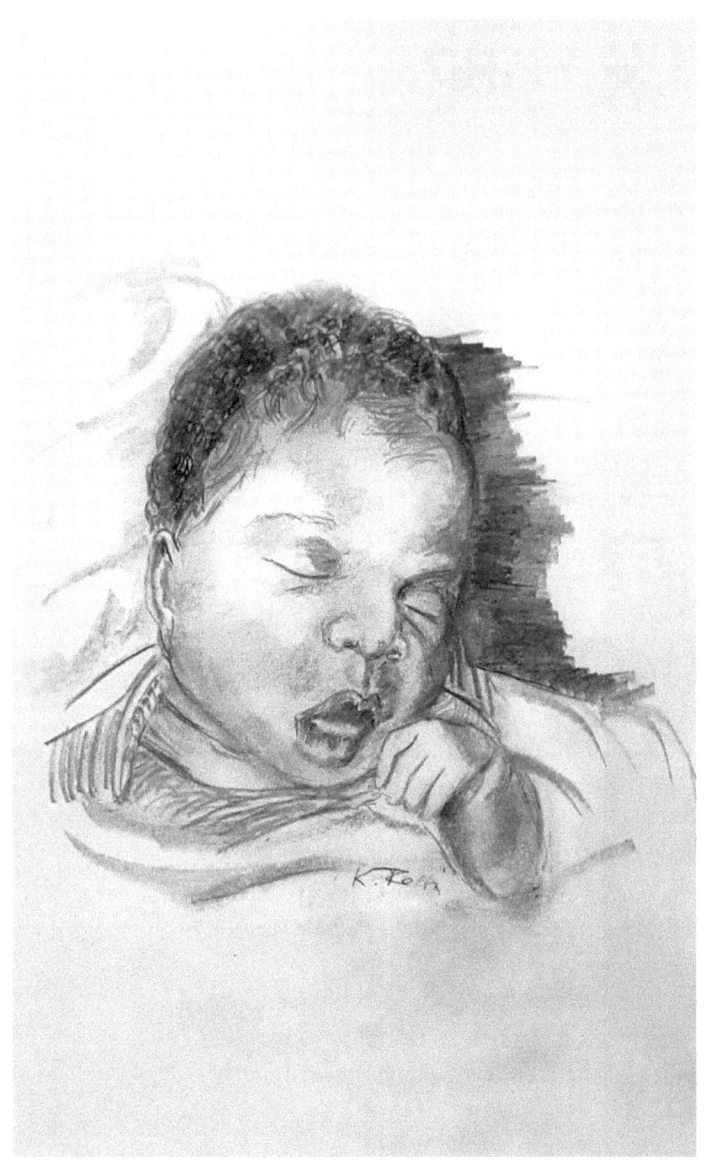

Sing With Me Across National Borders

(Suhani Jain)

I woke up in the morning early, saw the birds chirping
Which made me realize, how beautiful the world would be
If everyone of us could unite,
So, Sing with me across national borders
Let's make the Idea of a peaceful world happen

The days have passed and, left all of us with a heavy heart
Let's be each other's support and, let the negativity deport
So, Sing with me across national borders
Let's make the Idea of a peaceful world happen

When everyone thought, it's the end of the world
There were people who helped others, and cheered
What if everyone of us could make a positive impact,
And make the world a better place
So, Sing with me across national borders
Let's make the Idea of a peaceful world happen

Now, it feels like the night will be soon over,
The negative energy flow is becoming slower and slower
People are coming to each other's help, feels like the lost raven
is back
May the humanity be restored and peace spread
So, Sing with me across national borders
Let's make the Idea of a peaceful world happen

The Person I Want You To Be

(Yhohannah Holm)

If I had a chance to say something
I'd say hi, I'd say goodbye.
I'd say I wish you were a different person
I'd say I wish you were my friend
I'd say I wish this was the beginning
Not a horrible, dark dead end.
If I had a moment, if I could steal a glance
If I was allowed and if I had the chance
I'd say something's in my heart
But it's not the person you are
It's the person I wanted you to be.
when you were alone with me
I look in your eyes to see a lost man
Clingy and needy and looking
Looking for God in all the wrong places
Looking for love in all the wrong spaces
I look in your eyes and I see a joker
With a weird taste in humour
And I know you even wish you were a different person
You told me once and I can't love you
I love the person I want you to be
I love the person I want you to be
But that person doesn't exist.

I wasn't ready for this but I was
I wasn't ready to leave you but I was.

I just have to go back one more time
To make sure that I detest you
I think your absence is making me think
Making me cry
A sick cry.
Your arms were too tight around me
And your kisses too wet
Your effort to be near me too strong
Your love for me caused me trouble
Your love for me caused me pain
Your determination was a fired in your heart
It caused me to wake up in the morning
And say "What the hell was that?"
A time will come when you will come again
Will I detest you again?
I have to go back and see.

On The Roof Of The World

(Mladen M. Tokić)

Seeing it in people
no name
to love her in love
without a medal
bring her flowers
the most beautiful flowers
nameless
favorite year
without crime
my little one

Awaken her in stone
to hide the suffering of the century
thirsty to speak
say a thousand times
there you are beside me
in the oasis
of my little wild ones
golden-eyed butterflies
there you are
on this stingy
on this fast
on the roof of the world
right next to me
everyone is in heaven

About the poets in the poetry book

Arijit Misra (India)

Arijit Misra was born 1969, in Kolkata, Westbengal, India. "Love me as I am or watch me go..."

Aziza Dahdouh (Algeria)

Aziza Dahdouh, an Algerian teacher, poetess and photographer. She writes in English and Arabic. So far she has published two books: "Soul Of The Bird" and "Colors Of My Soul".

Michael Morrissey (USA/ Germany)

born 1946 in Washington, DC, living in Germany since 1977. Retired after teaching English at the University of Kassel for 25 years, author of several books, available on Amazon.

San Lin Tun (Myanmar)

born 1974, living in Yango, the former capital of Myanmar (Burma). "I am a bilingual freelance writer of prose an prosody and I write both, in English an Myanmar. I have published mor than ten English books so far. My recent novel "An English Writer" came out in 2019."

Gary Steven Corseri (USA)

born 1946 in New York City, living in Washington. "Details about the USA," he says, "would fill an encyclopedia; I'll just say: it's quite a stew!" His poems, articles and fiction have appeared at hundreds of international publications and websites, including City Lights Review, Countercurrents and The New York Times; he has performed his poems at the Carter Presidential Library; his dramas have been produced on PBS-Atlanta and in universities; he has published two novels and two collections of poetry and has taught in US public schools and prisons and in US and Japanese universities.

Milka Minkova (Macedonia)	(no further infomation)
Lyonga Micheal Justin Mushaga (Cameroon)	born 1999 in Kumba, Cameroon. "The mind is a powerful tool, so I use it for imagination an creativity."
Jillani Birech (Algeria)	born 1990, in Djelfa, Algeria. He is a teacher of English and comes from a small town called Djelfa in southern Algeria. Jillani holds a Master's Degree in English and enjoys literature and creative writing. He is an avid reader and a lifelong fan of the poetry genres. He wrote three English poetry books: Haikus in Hopefulness, Soul Reflections and Haikus in Esperanza (Spanish).
Christian Nae (Romania)	born 1964, published poems in magazines and in Anthologies. He is the author of the children's book "Dream Garden".
Sascha Helck (Germany)	born 1981 in Bremervörde, Germany. Poems and horror stories have accompanied him since childhood. What started with ghost stories turned into stories about vampires and zombics. In 2015 his horror novel "When the Graves Bleed" was published.
Devi Maya Pradhan (Bhutan)	born 2000, from Tsirang, Bhutan. Since a very young age, she had that zeal for writing. "It's deep inside me that keeps persuading me to write," she says. She is the recipients of various international awards in poetry.

Ishmail Kamara (Sierra Leone / West Africa)	Currently living in the Netherlands. Autor of two books, including his new novel "A hundred Golden Horses – a journey to the promised land."
Joanna Janosz (Poland)	born 1961. University education in Polish literature. Currently lives in England, work as carrier for disabled people.
Keith Hyland (Ireland)	comes from Ireland/ Dublin.
Lucia V. Cleaeno (Netherlands)	"My parents gave me the name of bright, Lucia. My character is an unpredictable source for my writings. Alike the erratic, unpredictable Dutch North Sea riptide, my place of birth. Myths and ancient narratives are the chisels to sculpture my tales."
Laseeta Kunhikannan (India)	(no further infomation)
Melissa Emalia Medina (Puerto Rico / USA)	Melissa Medina AKA Emalia was born in Rio Piedras, Puerto Rico, and raised in Spanish Harlem, NYC. She is a poet, writer, and author of Alpha Omega Poetry: Life Lessons, and How wildcats and wolves became cats and dogs, a children's book written in poetic form.
Yhohannah Holm	(no further infomation)
Suhani Jain (India)	born 2000, " I live in Dhar district of Madhya Pradesh state of India. I'm a small town girl studying engineering and sometimes I try to convey what I feel through my words and singing out loud."

Samar Bhowmick (Bangladesh)	Born in 1971 into an aristocratic Hindu family in the Kishoreganj district, Bangladesh, the youngest of eight siblings. He loved poetry since childhood. He made his debut in the school magazine. His writing has already found recognition at home and abroad. Its main theme is love and humanity. The "ANU" of a poet who believes in a being is its main pillar. He told everything to the only "ANU". Anu is his love, paramatma, water, soil, light, air and parameshwar.
Mladen M. Tokić (Bosna i Hercegovina)	Mladen M. Tokić, poet, writer and journalist, has been writing poetry since his early youth. He published poetry in the former state of Yugoslavia, mainly in literary magazines for art - culture - literature. He was a journalist for many written and electronic media in the period 1995-2000. Today, retired Mladen has returned to his old love of poetry. He is represented in several collections of international poetry, and he understands poetry as a way of life.

Table Of Contents

About The Author

Kris Felti, born in Dresden in 1965 as the first of the two twin girls, grew up in the country, where horse riding and plundering fruit trees were still quite normal pastimes. As a teenager she began to write her own texts. She is now the mother of three grown children and is once again devoting herself to her first great love: writing. She has a degree in engineering and a degree in computer science. So far she has published the children's book "Gänseblümchen und ihre außergewöhnlichen Freunde" in German, the volume of poetry "Du bist mein Ich - Sehnsucht" in English and German, and the children's book "Daisy" in Arabic..

www.krisfelti-buch-und-lyrik.com

Zeitfracht Medien GmbH
Ferdinand-Jühlke-Straße 7
99095 Erfurt, Deutschland
produktsicherheit@kolibri360.de